The Rainy Day Adventure

tiger tales

Little Elephant and
Little Tiger were
playing in the jungle,
when
SPLISH,
   SPLOSH,
      SPLASH!
It began to rain.
"We can keep dry
under that tree," said
Little Tiger.

But Little Elephant was
too big. His front half
was dry, but his backside
was still out in the rain!

He tried facing the other way,
but then his head was wet.
"Never mind," said Little Tiger.
"Let's go to the cave."

Little Tiger raced through the
rain, with Little Elephant splashing
along behind him.
"We're nearly there!" shouted
Little Tiger.

But when they
arrived they found two
bears already there.

"Go away!" shouted the biggest bear.
"We were here first."
Little Tiger didn't argue, because
he knew of an even better place.

They splashed through
the rain until they came
to a big rock.

Little Elephant squeezed under the
rock next to Little Tiger. But as he did,
he pushed Little Tiger out the other side.

"Thanks a lot, Little Tiger," said Little Elephant. "I'm dry at last."

"But I'm soaking wet," said Little Tiger. "Move over!"

Little Elephant shifted his bottom and curled up his trunk, but there was still not enough room for the two of them.

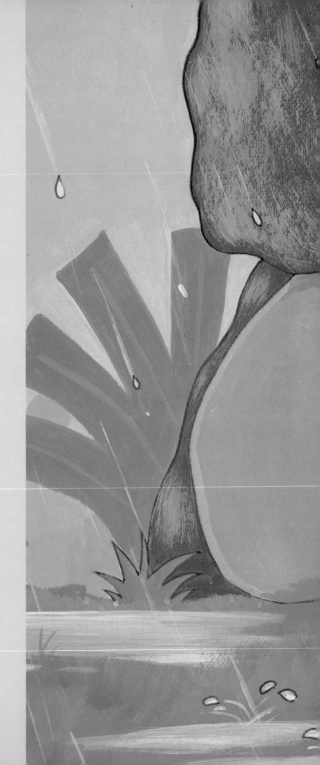

They raced through the
rain until they reached Little
Tiger's favorite fallen tree.

Little Tiger crawled underneath.
But poor Little Elephant couldn't
even get his head inside!

"Can't you think of anywhere else?" said Little Elephant. He was very wet now.

"I know!" shouted Little Tiger. "We can stay dry under the mango tree."

But when they got there, they found a
family of monkeys had already arrived.

"Come on in," chattered the monkeys.
"There's plenty of room."

But there wasn't enough
room for the monkeys as well.

"There's another cave by the river," said Little Tiger. So SPLISH, SPLOSH! Off they went to the river.

Suddenly Little Elephant skidded into Little Tiger,
and they both fell into the river.
"We're wetter than ever!" cried Little Elephant.

"But it's fun though!" said Little Tiger.
They were having so much fun that they didn't even notice when the rain stopped and the sun came out.

Little Tiger character taken from the series of books
by Julie Sykes and Tim Warnes
Illustrations by Czes Pachela, based on
the characters created by Tim Warnes

tiger tales
an imprint of ME Media LLC
202 Old Ridgefield Road
Wilton, CT 06897
First Published in Great Britain 2001
by Little Tiger Press, London
© 2001 Little Tiger Press
Printed in Singapore
ISBN 1-58925-362-0